12 REASONS TO LOVE THE
ST. LOUIS CARDINALS

by Marty Gitlin

12 STORY LIBRARY

www.12StoryLibrary.com

12-Story Library is an imprint of Peterson Publishing Company and Press Room Editions.

Produced for 12-Story Library by Red Line Editorial

Photographs ©: Chris Lee/St. Louis Post-Dispatch/AP Images, cover, 1; Bettmann/Corbis, 4, 5, 6, 7, 11; Bruno Torres/Bettmann/Corbis, 9; AP Images, 13, 14, 17; Gene Puskar/ AP Images, 15; R. Gino Santa Maria/Shutterstock Images, 18, 24, 28, 29; Joseph Sohm/ Shutterstock Images, 19; Jeff Roberson/AP Images, 21, 22; Eric Gay/AP Images, 23; Jerry Naunheim Jr./AP Images, 25

ISBN
978-1-63235-217-0 (hardcover)
978-1-63235-244-6 (paperback)
978-1-62143-269-2 (hosted ebook)

Library of Congress Control Number: 2015934322

Printed in the United States of America
Mankato, MN
October, 2015

Go beyond the book. Get free, up-to-date content on this topic at 12StoryLibrary.com.

TABLE OF CONTENTS

HITTING MACHINE ROGERS HORNSBY IS BEST WITH A BAT

Baseball fans in the early 1920s did not have to wonder who was going to lead the National League (NL) in hitting. They knew St. Louis Cardinals slugger Rogers Hornsby would probably finish well ahead of the pack.

The Texas native posted the highest batting average in the league every season from 1920 to 1925. But he was not just a singles hitter. He paced the NL in doubles four times, averaging 42 per year. He twice led the league in home runs. And he had the most runs batted in (RBIs) four times. His .424 batting average in 1924 still ranks as the second best for one season in Major League Baseball (MLB).

Rogers Hornsby swings at a pitch in 1917.

Hornsby was also part of the Cardinals' first World Series win. They beat the New York Yankees in 1926.

Hornsby thought about nothing but baseball—even when the snow was falling. "People ask me what I do in winter when there's no baseball," he once said. "I'll tell you what I do. I stare out the window and wait for spring."

When spring rolled around, he was ready. He used his bat like a magic wand. His .358 career batting average is second in the history of the sport.

2

Seasons in which Rogers Hornsby led the NL in batting average, home runs, and RBIs. That's called the Triple Crown.

- Hornsby played all the infield positions but was mostly a second baseman.
- He played with four other teams, including the St. Louis Browns from 1933 to 1937.
- He was inducted into the Baseball Hall of Fame in 1942.

THINK ABOUT IT

What are the qualities a baseball player needs to be a great hitter? Which of those skills are physical? Which ones are mental and emotional?

THE GAS HOUSE GANG WINS IT ALL

The Great Depression hit the United States in 1929. Life was hard for many Americans over the next decade. Money was tight. Luxuries were few. In St. Louis, a team known as "The Gas House Gang" lifted spirits in 1934.

Daffy Dean (left) and Dizzy Dean in 1934

The Cardinals earned that nickname for their wacky personalities and rough play. Their stars were also given colorful nicknames. Their top hitters were Joe "Ducky" Medwick, Johnny "Pepper" Martin, and James Anthony "Ripper" Collins. Their best pitchers were brothers Jay "Dizzy" Dean and Paul "Daffy" Dean.

"They don't look like a major league ball club," wrote sportswriter Frank Graham of the *New York Sun*. "Their uniforms are stained and dirty. . . .

They spit out of the sides of their mouths. . . . They are not afraid of anybody."

The 1934 Cardinals closed out the regular season strong. They beat the Cincinnati Reds in four straight games to win the NL pennant. Then they captured the World Series title.

Dizzy Dean shut out the Detroit Tigers in Game 7. But the Gas House Gang will always be remembered for more than their success on the field.

Dizzy Dean plays a tuba at the ballpark in 1934.

DANDY DIZZY DEAN

The Cardinals of the 1920s and 1930s boasted many great players. But none was better or more colorful than pitcher Dizzy Dean. He averaged 26 wins a year from 1933 to 1936. He peaked in 1934. Dean had a 30–7 record and won the NL Most Valuable Player (MVP) Award. He would also mock opposing hitters. He sometimes laughed at them when they struck out.

799
Runs scored by the Cardinals in 1934 to lead the NL.

- St. Louis finished with a record of 95–58.
- Ripper Collins led the Cardinals in batting average (.333), home runs (35), and RBIs (128).
- Dizzy Dean led the team in wins (30), earned-run average (2.66), and strikeouts (195).

STAN IS THE MAN FOR THE CARDINALS

Stan Musial's nickname is a simple one. He is known as "Stan the Man." It's fitting. He is "the man" in Cardinals baseball history.

Although he began as a pitcher, Musial became one of the greatest sluggers ever. He won seven batting titles. He led the NL in doubles eight times. He also topped the NL in triples and runs five times each. It's no wonder that he won the NL MVP Award three times. Musial was elected into the Baseball Hall of Fame in 1969.

Musial remained a force at an age when most players have long retired. He even batted .330 in 1962 at the age of 41. His epic major league career began in 1941 and ended in 1963. He stayed in St. Louis for the entire time.

Musial enjoyed one of the longest and greatest careers in the history of baseball. Yet he is remembered for more than his skills. Musial always played fair. Off the field, he was gracious to fans. No player is more symbolic of Cardinals baseball than Stan "The Man" Musial.

1
Season, in 1945, that Stan Musial missed while serving in the US Navy in World War II.

- Musial and the Cardinals won World Series titles in 1942, 1944, and 1946.
- He was awarded the Presidential Medal of Freedom in 2011.
- A statue of Musial greets fans outside Busch Stadium.

Stan Musial speaks to fans at Busch Stadium prior to his last game in 1963.

4

GIBSON STANDS OUT IN "THE YEAR OF THE PITCHER"

The 1968 season was known as "The Year of the Pitcher." Many pitchers around MLB had great seasons. Yet none was as dominant as Bob Gibson. The Cardinals' right-handed hurler had one of the best pitching seasons of all time.

Gibson crafted a 1.12 earned-run average (ERA) that year. It still stands as the best ERA since the Dead Ball Era ended in 1919. His 13 shutouts were the most by any pitcher in nearly 100 years. He won 22 games. He led St. Louis to its second straight pennant. He easily won the NL Cy Young Award as the league's best pitcher. But Gibson also won the NL MVP Award. That's usually given to a hitter.

His success began with his fierce nature on the mound. Gibson sometimes intimidated batters by throwing his wicked fastball within inches of their heads. But his control

A NEW PLACE TO PLAY

The Cardinals won the World Series in 1964 and 1967. But they did not call the same stadium home in both seasons. They played at Sportsman's Park for 47 years. That field, later called Busch Stadium I, could fit only 30,000 fans. The team moved in 1966 to Busch Stadium II. It had 50,000 seats. Fans flocked to the new ballpark in 1967. The Cardinals set a team record (since broken) by drawing more than 2 million fans that season.

was so pinpoint that he rarely hit them.

Gibson led the way in 1968, but many pitchers were great. They were so good, in fact, that MLB lowered the mound the next year. Doing so gave batters a better chance for success at the plate.

268

Strikeouts recorded by Bob Gibson in 1968.

- Gibson led the Cardinals to World Series titles in 1964 and 1967.
- Over his career, Gibson won 251 games and had a 2.91 ERA.
- He won nine straight Gold Gloves from 1965 to 1973 as the NL's top fielding pitcher.

Bob Gibson throws the first pitch of the 1968 World Series.

LOU BROCK SWIPES 118 BASES

The Cardinals opened the 1974 season against the Pittsburgh Pirates on April 5. Speedster Lou Brock led off the bottom of the sixth inning with a single to center field. Then, as he was known to do, he took off for second. Brock raced for the bag. He was tagged out. It would be the last time in a while.

Brock wasn't caught stealing again until May 21. By then he had 28 stolen bases. And he kept going. Brock stole 11 more bases before he was caught again on June 10. He was on pace to set the single-season record. It was around that time that Brock really turned it on.

"It's like trying to keep water from going over the dam," said New York Mets pitcher Harry Parker one night.

"You know what's coming, but you're powerless."

Brock did not just break the all-time mark of 104 stolen bases. He destroyed it. He finished the season with 118. It still stands as a NL record. However, the Oakland Athletics' Rickey Henderson stole 130 bases in 1982.

8

Seasons in which Lou Brock led the NL in stolen bases.

- Brock began his career with the Chicago Cubs.
- The Cardinals traded for Brock during the 1964 season.
- Brock played 16 seasons in St. Louis.
- He was a member of the 1964 and 1967 World Series championship teams.

Lou Brock successfully steals third base against the Chicago Cubs in May 1974.

THINK ABOUT IT

Teams attempted to steal bases more often during Lou Brock's era than they do today. Why do you think that's the case? What are some of the benefits to trying to steal a lot of bases? What are some of the pitfalls?

THE WIZARD OF OZ BACKFLIP

Fans did not want to arrive late for any Cardinals game from 1982 to 1996. If they did, they would miss quite a show from acrobatic shortstop Ozzie Smith.

Smith jumped and dived to make plays all over the field. He was such a superb fielder that he earned the nickname "Wizard of Oz." And on special occasions, he thrilled fans in another way. Before the first and last games of the season, he did a backflip as he arrived at his position in the first inning.

A WAGER WITH WHITEY

Cardinals manager Whitey Herzog wanted Ozzie Smith to hit more ground balls rather than fly balls. That would allow Smith to use his great speed to beat out base hits. So Herzog approached Smith with a message. Every time Smith hit a fly ball, he had to pay Herzog a dollar. When Smith hit a ground ball, Herzog paid him a dollar. By July of that season, Smith was already up $300. Herzog called off the deal after that.

Ozzie Smith performs his famous backflip before a 1985 World Series game.

Ozzie Smith turns a double play against the San Francisco Giants in the 1987 playoffs.

The backflip tradition began in 1978. Smith played for the San Diego Padres at the time. He began doing flips in practices. Before the final home game that season, he performed one in front of the fans. The crowd went wild. It became a tradition the next year.

Smith was a weak hitter early in his career. But he worked to become a good one. He peaked in 1987, batting .303 with 104 runs scored. He placed second in the NL MVP voting that season.

13
Gold Glove Awards won by Ozzie Smith during his career.

- Smith was known for his defense but became a good hitter, too.
- He ended his career with 2,460 hits and 589 stolen bases.
- Smith helped the Cardinals win the 1982 World Series.

JACK BUCK TELLS CARDINALS FANS TO "GO CRAZY"

It was Game 5 of the 1985 NL Championship Series (NLCS). The site was Busch Stadium in St. Louis. The series between the Cardinals and Los Angeles Dodgers was tied at 2–2. So was the game. St. Louis was batting with one out in the bottom of the ninth inning.

Up to the plate stepped Cardinals shortstop Ozzie Smith. The count was one ball, two strikes. Los Angeles pitcher Tom Niedenfuer fired a fastball inside. Smith sent the ball over the right-field fence. The home run gave the Cardinals an important win. The blast also prompted one of the most famous radio calls ever. St. Louis announcer Jack Buck screamed out to everyone listening, "Go crazy, folks, go crazy!" And they did.

Most amazing is that Smith only hit 28 home runs in his 19-year career. St. Louis clinched the pennant by winning the next game. But it lost to the Kansas City Royals in the World Series.

11

World Series titles won by the Cardinals through 2014.

- Only the New York Yankees, with 27, have won more.
- The Cardinals have 19 NL pennants.
- The New York/San Francisco Giants have 23 NL pennants but only eight World Series titles.

Ozzie Smith rounds the bases after his game-winning home run in Game 5 of the 1985 NLCS.

FANS GAZE OUT AT THE GATEWAY ARCH

St. Louis fans can see many beautiful sights from the stands at the new Busch Stadium. They can see the plush green grass in the infield and outfield. They can see the big, colorful scoreboard in right-center field. They can see the tall light towers that make night games possible.

But the most majestic landmark is not inside the stadium. It can be seen beyond the center-field seats. It is the famous Gateway Arch. The stainless steel monument is the tallest arch in the world. It stands 630 feet (192 m) tall. Visitors can look out from the top of the Arch and see 30 miles (48 km) on a clear day. It is the highest point in downtown St. Louis.

Busch Stadium III in St. Louis opened in 2006.

Busch Stadium II

The Gateway Arch was completed in 1965, just a year before the opening of the second Busch Stadium.

1,076
Steps from the bottom to the top of the Gateway Arch.

- The Arch was built from 1963 to 1965.
- It symbolizes that St. Louis is the "Gateway to the West."

THE NEW BUSCH STADIUM

The Cardinals have played in Busch Stadium since 1953. But there have been different Busch Stadiums over the years. In 1953, Sportsman's Park in St. Louis became Busch Stadium I. A new Busch Stadium was built in 1966. Today's Busch Stadium opened in 2006. It was built next to the old ballpark. The first game in the new Busch Stadium was played on April 10. Slugger Albert Pujols blasted a home run as the Cardinals beat the Milwaukee Brewers 6–4.

WATCHING ALBERT WAS ABSOLUTELY AWESOME

Few expected Albert Pujols to become a baseball superstar. The Cardinals picked him in the 1999 draft. But they waited until the 13th round. More than 400 players were selected before him. The Cardinals quickly learned they had made a good pick.

Pujols debuted in the Cardinals starting lineup in 2001. He destroyed NL pitching from the start. He batted .370 with eight home runs and 27 RBIs in April. And he did not stop clobbering the baseball for St. Louis for more than a decade.

Pujols emerged as the greatest Cardinals slugger since Stan Musial. He led the NL in runs scored five times. He was voted NL MVP in 2005, 2008, and 2009. He batted at least .300, drove in at least 100 runs, and hit at least 30 home runs every year from 2001 to 2010. And he nearly did so again in 2011. He hit .299 with 99 RBIs and 37 home runs. Pujols was so consistent that fans called him "The Machine."

10

Seasons, in an 11-year span, in which Albert Pujols placed in the top five in NL MVP voting. The run lasted from 2001 through 2011.

- Pujols was born in Santo Domingo, Dominican Republic.
- He played for the Cardinals from 2001 through 2011.
- He played outfield and third base before settling as a first baseman in 2004.
- In 2012, Pujols signed with the Los Angeles Angels.

Mike Matheny became the Cardinals manager in 2012. Before then he was a Cardinals catcher and teammate of Pujols. Even Matheny marveled at Pujols's hitting skills. "I wonder if he knows how difficult it is for the rest of us?" Matheny said in 2003.

ALBERT AND STAN

Albert Pujols became the face of the Cardinals in the 2000s. But even Pujols looked up to Stan Musial. The two stars became friends during Pujols's time in St. Louis. Pujols admired Musial's graciousness and friendliness. "He blessed my life and many, many lives in baseball," Pujols said after Musial died in 2013.

Albert Pujols blasts a home run against the Milwaukee Brewers in 2009.

CARDINALS WIN A WILD WORLD SERIES IN 2011

The Cardinals met the Texas Rangers on October 27, 2011, at Busch Stadium. It was Game 6 of the World Series. A win would give the Rangers the crown. And they were on the verge of clinching it. But St. Louis third baseman David Freese smashed a triple to tie it with two out in the ninth inning.

The Rangers then went ahead 9–7 in the 10th inning. The Cardinals again appeared doomed. But again they rallied with two outs to tie it. The fans in the stands and millions watching on TV knew they were seeing history.

David Freese hits a game-winning home run in Game 6 of the 2011 World Series.

Cardinals teammates celebrate with David Freese as he arrives at home plate at the end of Game 6 of the 2011 World Series.

Freese stepped to the plate with the game still tied in the eleventh. Texas pitcher Mark Lowe delivered a fastball. Freese took a mighty swing. *Smack!* He launched the baseball over the center-field fence for a home run. The Cardinals had won a classic. They then won Game 7 to take the title.

THINK ABOUT IT

Baseball experts debate whether players are good in the clutch. That means they perform well in high-pressure situations. Do you think players perform differently—better or worse—in clutch situations? Use evidence to support your answer.

3

Home runs by Albert Pujols in Game 3 of the 2011 World Series.

- Pujols had five hits, six RBIs, and four runs in the game.
- Game 6 hero David Freese was named World Series MVP.
- Of Freese's eight World Series hits, only three were singles.

23

ST. LOUIS HAS THE BEST FANS IN THE LAND

In 2014, more than 3.5 million fans streamed into Busch Stadium to watch the Cardinals. Nearly every game was sold out. The team attracted at least 3 million fans every year but one from 1998 to 2014. No MLB team enjoyed more support. Cardinals games also drew the top TV ratings in the sport.

It's clear the people of St. Louis love their Cardinals. But many players appreciate the Cardinals fans, too. St. Louis fans are considered to be the most knowledgeable about the sport and their team. They are known for always cheering for good plays—even if the other team made the play.

There's no way to truly measure which team has the best fans. That didn't stop Forbes from trying in 2015. It found that the Cardinals have the most local fans of any MLB team. That is especially impressive

Mascot Fredbird pumps up fans at Busch Stadium.

Cardinals fans celebrate the team's 2011 World Series championship.

because 23 MLB teams play in bigger cities.

"I have never seen one city so proudly bear the local team's colors," ESPN sportswriter Jim Caple wrote.

43,712
Average attendance for Cardinals games at Busch Stadium in 2014.

- In 2014, 76 percent of people in St. Louis attended, watched, or listened to a Cardinals game.
- More than 3.54 million fans attended Cardinals home games that year, second in MLB.

POWERFUL KMOX RADIO

Before fans watched baseball on TV, they listened to games on the radio. No radio station gave more fans access to a team than KMOX in St. Louis. Its powerful signal and middle-of-the-country location allowed it to reach radios throughout the nation. Many people not living near St. Louis became fans of the Cardinals because they could listen to their broadcasts. KMOX began regularly carrying St. Louis games in 1927. It is still the home of Cardinals baseball.

MOLINA MAKES HIS MARK

Some catchers hit well but are weak defensively. Other catchers are fine on defense but hit poorly. Then there is Cardinals catcher Yadier Molina. He can do it all.

"The game has never seen a better catcher than Yadier Molina," longtime Cardinals manager Tony La Russa said.

Some might disagree. But there is no doubt Molina is one of the game's best catchers today. Molina debuted with the Cardinals in 2004. He wasn't immediately a star. Before long he became one, though. Molina's defense shined first. Few balls got past him. Potential base-stealers had to think twice. Molina became one of baseball's best at throwing out runners. His caught-stealing percentage soared. He ranked among the NL's top three

every year but one from 2005 to 2014.

Before long, Molina began thriving on offense, too. He batted over .300 four times from 2008 to 2013. He slammed 22 home runs in 2012 and 44 doubles in 2013. From 2009 through 2014, Molina made the All-Star Game and won a Gold Glove every year.

12
Stolen bases recorded by Yadier Molina in 2012. That was a career high.

- Molina was born in Bayamon, Puerto Rico.
- His brothers Bengie Molina and Jose Molina also were major league catchers.
- He finished in the top four in NL MVP voting in 2012 and 2013.

Yadier Molina prepares to throw out a runner in a 2014 game.

12 KEY DATES

1892
The Cardinals join the NL as the St. Louis Browns. They become the Cardinals in 1900.

1926
Behind star infielder Rogers Hornsby, the Cardinals win their first World Series. They beat Babe Ruth and the New York Yankees in seven games.

1934
A Cardinals team nicknamed "The Gas House Gang" wins the World Series with great play and great flair on the field.

1937
Joe "Ducky" Medwick wins the coveted Triple Crown by leading the NL with a .374 bating average, 31 home runs, and 154 RBIs.

1945
Superstar Stan "The Man" Musial misses the season to serve in World War II. It is the only season from 1941 to 1963 in which the Cardinals legend did not suit up for the team.

1968
Right-hander Bob Gibson has a 1.12 ERA, the best in MLB since the Dead Ball Era. The record-setting season comes after Gibson helped the Cardinals win the 1964 and 1967 World Series.

1974
Lou Brock steals 118 bases for the Cardinals, setting a major league record that would last for eight years.

1982
Star shortstop Ozzie Smith and the Cardinals beat the Milwaukee Brewers to win the World Series.

1998
Cardinals first baseman Mark McGwire hits 70 home runs, shattering the previous record of 61. However, he later admitted to using performance-enhancing drugs that season.

2001
Slugger Albert Pujols debuts and begins a 10-year streak in which he hits at least .300 with 30 home runs and 100 RBIs. He wins three NL MVP Awards in that time.

2006
The Cardinals' new Busch Stadium opens in downtown St. Louis. It features sweeping views of the city skyline and the Gateway Arch.

2011
Third baseman David Freese triples to save the Cardinals from elimination in Game 6 of the World Series. His walk-off homer wins the game in the 11th inning. The Cardinals go on to win their NL-record 11th World Series title in Game 7 over the Texas Rangers.

GLOSSARY

clutch
Situations in which there is a lot of pressure on a team, often because the game is on the line.

consistent
Able to do the same thing over and over at a similar quality.

Dead Ball Era
A period from 1900 to 1919 in which MLB pitchers dominated.

ERA
The average number of runs a pitcher gives up over nine innings.

gracious
Polite, respectful, and pleasant.

landmark
An easily identifiable object or structure.

majestic
Impressive and beautiful.

mock
To tease or make fun of someone.

pennant
A league championship in baseball.

shutout
A pitched game in which the opponent does not score.

FOR MORE INFORMATION

Books

Frisch, Aaron. *St. Louis Cardinals.* Mankato, MN: The Creative Company, 2011.

Gitlin, Marty. *St. Louis Cardinals.* Edina, MN: Abdo Publishing, 2011.

Hawkins, Jeff. *World Series.* Minneapolis, MN: Abdo Publishing, 2013.

Websites

Cardinals Kids Club
stlouis.cardinals.mlb.com/stl/fan_forum/kidsclub.jsp

MLB.com: Kids
mlb.mlb.com/mlb/kids

St. Louis Cardinals
stlouis.cardinals.mlb.com/index.jsp?c_id=stl

INDEX

About the Author

Marty Gitlin is a freelance writer based in Cleveland, Ohio. He has written nearly 100 educational books, including many about sports. Gitlin has won more than 45 awards during his 25 years as a writer, including first place for general excellence from the Associated Press. He lives with his wife and three children.

READ MORE FROM 12-STORY LIBRARY

Every 12-Story Library book is available in many formats, including Amazon Kindle and Apple iBooks. For more information, visit your device's store or 12StoryLibrary.com.